Grammar Builder

Level 2
English

First edition 2013

ISBN 978-981-07-5257-6

Welcome to studySMART !

Grammar Builder lets your child review and apply essential grammar rules.

Knowledge of grammar is essential in ensuring your child understands the patterns and rules in the English language. As your child progresses through the practice worksheets, he will strengthen the skills needed to read and write well.

Grammar items covered in one level are reinforced at the subsequent level. This helps to ensure that your child consolidates his learning of a particular grammar item and builds upon it.

Each grammar item is covered in three pages. The first two pages target your child's ability to identify and apply the grammar item. The third page provides a quick assessment of your child's understanding of the use of the grammar item. A revision section at the end of the book also allows for easy assessment of your child's understanding of the grammar items covered in each workbook.

How to use this book?

1. Introduce the target grammar item at the top of the page to your child.

2. Direct your child's attention to the grammar box to review the grammar rule.

3. Let your child complete the practices independently.

4. Use the Assessment pages and Revision section to evaluate your child's understanding of the grammar items.

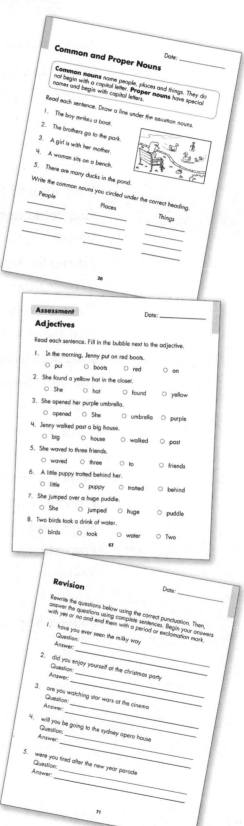

3

Contents

Date: _____

Telling Sentences and Questions

A **telling sentence** tells something. It begins with a capital letter and ends with a period. A **question** asks something. It begins with a capital letter and ends with a question mark.

Read each sentence. Write *T* on the line if the sentence is a telling sentence. Write *Q* on the line if it is a question.

1. I took my pet to see the vet. _____

2. Was your pet sick? _____

3. What did the vet do? _____

4. The vet checked my pet. _____

5. The vet said my pet had a cold. _____

6. Is your pet well now? _____

7. My pet is well now. _____

Telling Sentences and Questions

Read each sentence. Decide if it is a telling sentence or a question. Then, copy each sentence or question correctly on the line. Remember to use capital letters and the correct punctuation.

1. where is James

   _____

2. James is in the classroom

   _____

3. he is helping Miss Lina clean the board

   _____

4. who is the one sweeping the floor

   _____

5. that is Monica

   _____

6. she is our class monitor

   _____

Date: _____

Telling Sentences and Questions

Look at the underlined part of each sentence. If it is written correctly, fill in the last bubble. If not, fill in the bubble next to the correct answer.

1. <u>The girl</u> likes rabbits.

   ○ The Girl
   ○ the girl
   ○ correct as is

2. The boy likes <u>cats?</u>

   ○ cats.
   ○ cats
   ○ correct as is

3. <u>do you</u> have a pet?

   ○ Do you
   ○ Do You
   ○ correct as is

4. <u>He has</u> a bird.

   ○ Has he
   ○ he has
   ○ correct as is

5. <u>What kind</u> of bird is it?

   ○ What Kind
   ○ what kind
   ○ correct as is

6. I like <u>cats.</u>

   ○ Cats.
   ○ cats?
   ○ correct as is

7. What pet do you <u>like.</u>

   ○ like?
   ○ Like?
   ○ correct as is

8. I want a <u>hamster.</u>

   ○ Hamster?
   ○ hamster?
   ○ correct as is

Yes / No Questions and Answers

Yes / No questions are answered with a **yes** or **no**, or with the question written as a statement.

Answer the following questions by writing *yes* or *no* in the blanks.

1. Did you eat breakfast this morning?

    _____, I did.

2. Are you wearing a new watch?

    _____, I am.

3. Do you want some honey with your waffles?

    _____, I want some honey with my waffles.

4. Is Kay going with you?

    _____, Kay is not going with me.

5. Can you give the cap to Jon when you see him?

    _____, I can give the cap to Jon when I see him.

6. Will you be home for tea?

    _____, I will not be home for tea.

Yes / No Questions and Answers

Write suitable questions to the answers given.

1. _____

   Yes, I want to visit Grandma this weekend.

2. _____

   No, I will not be going swimming.

3. _____

   Yes, the book is interesting.

4. _____

   Yes, I would like to pet your dog.

5. _____

   No, I did not see Benson at lunch.

6. _____

   Yes, we shall have pizza tomorrow evening.

7. _____

   No, Jaden has not gone home yet.

8. _____

   Yes, you should turn off the light.

Yes / No Questions and Answers

Answer the following questions by writing *yes* or *no* statements.

E.g. Should Mandy go in now? (Yes)

Yes, Mandy should go in now.

1. Shall we celebrate Mom's birthday? (Yes)

    _____

2. Will you be watching the football game? (No)

    _____

3. Is Carlson going to Vancouver with his parents? (Yes)

    _____

4. Are you listening to the radio? (No)

    _____

5. Is there any milk in the refrigerator? (Yes)

    _____

6. May I speak to Mr Raye, please? (Yes)

    _____

Capitalizing Holidays and Events

> Holidays and events are proper nouns. Their names need to be capitalized.

Capitalize the holidays and events in the following statements or questions.

1. The first day of January is new year's day.

    _____

2. What special dish do we eat during thanksgiving?

    _____

3. Our school celebrates teacher's day with a party.

    _____

4. I am preparing a scary-looking costume for halloween.

    _____

5. Did you play tricks on your friends on april fool's day?

    _____

6. They are decorating the house for christmas.

    _____

Capitalizing Holidays and Events

Rewrite the sentences by replacing the underlined words with the correct event or holiday from the box.

Chinese New Year	Children's Day	Father's Day
Mother's Day	National Day	New Year's Eve

1. On <u>the day we honor mothers</u>, I will give my mother roses.

   _____

2. There is no school on <u>the day we honor children</u>.

   _____

3. We will have a party on <u>the day before New Year's Day</u>.

   _____

4. I will make breakfast for my father on <u>the day we honor fathers</u>.

   _____

5. On <u>our nation's birthday</u>, we fly our country's flag.

   _____

6. On <u>the day Chinese celebrate the lunar new year</u>, there will be fireworks.

   _____

Capitalizing Holidays and Events

Read the paragraph below. Copy it correctly on the lines. Remember to capitalize the names of holidays and events.

"What's wrong, Danny?" asked Trey. Danny said gloomily, "My dad was going to take me to the superbowl, but now he can't. He is going to the arizona international conference and will not be back in time!"

"Cheer up. Why don't you come over for dinner on good friday? You can stay over till easter!" grinned Trey.

_____

_____

_____

_____

_____

_____

_____

Exclamatory Sentences

An **exclamatory sentence** shows strong feelings such as excitement, surprise or fear. It ends with an exclamation mark (!).

Read each sentence. Circle each exclamation mark. Draw a line under the capital letter at the beginning of each sentence.

1. Help! The rat is on top!

2. Get the cat! It is trying to catch the fish!

3. That is great! We won!

Read each pair of sentences. Draw a line under the exclamatory sentence.

4. Oh my! The whole house is wet!

    The house is wet.

5. Run! They are catching up!

    They are catching up.

6. Surprise! Happy Birthday!

    We want to wish you a happy birthday.

Exclamatory Sentences

Choose the sentence in each pair that shows strong feelings. Write it on the line. Put an exclamation mark at the end.

1. Run to the show   We will go to the show

   _____

2. I'm late for it   Oh my, I'm very late

   _____

3. What a great show   I liked the show

   _____

4. The floor is wet   Watch out, the floor is wet

   _____

5. We had fun   Wow, we had lots of fun

   _____

Date: _____

Exclamatory Sentences

Read each group of sentences. Fill in the bubble next to the sentence or sentences that show strong feelings.

1. ○ The cow is on the hill.
    ○ Does the cow like grass?
    ○ Yes! The cow gave birth to a calf!

2. ○ Oh no! There is a rat in my house!
    ○ The rat is in my house.
    ○ Where is the rat?

3. ○ That boy is so naughty!
    ○ That boy is my brother.
    ○ Who is that boy?

4. ○ The pot can get hot.
    ○ The pot is hot!
    ○ Fill up the pot with hot water.

5. ○ There is a hole in the ground.
    ○ Did you see the hole in the ground?
    ○ Watch out! There is a hole in the ground!

6. ○ That baby cries so loudly!
    ○ The baby is crying.
    ○ Stop that baby from crying!

Exclamations and Commands

An **exclamation** shows strong feelings. It begins with a capital letter and ends with an exclamation mark (!). A **command** makes a request or tells someone to do something. It ends with a period.

Read each sentence. Write *E* if the sentence is an exclamation. Write *C* if the sentence is a command.

1. Look at these two dresses. _____

2. They're exactly the same! _____

3. Show them the matching shoes. _____

4. They look great! I love them! _____

5. You are amazing! _____

Write each sentence correctly.

6. (exclamation)   be yourself

_____

7. (command)   copy this page ten times

_____

Exclamations and Commands

Read each exclamation. Use words from the box to tell what strong feeling it shows.

excitement	fear	anger	surprise

1. I lost my jacket. I'll be so cold! _____

2. Look what I have! _____

3. I didn't know you had my jacket! _____

4. Give it to me now! _____

Look at the pictures. Underline the command that goes with each picture.

5. Change out of your clothes now.
    Put on your clothes now.

6. Keep quiet.
    You're so noisy!

Exclamations and Commands

Read each exclamation or command. Fill in the bubble next to the correct way to write it.

1. ○ you are my best friend in the world!
   ○ You are my best friend in the world!
   ○ you are my best friend in the world.

2. ○ The picture is beautiful!
   ○ The picture is beautiful.
   ○ the picture is beautiful!

3. ○ We did it!
   ○ we did it!
   ○ we did it.

4. ○ Teach me how to hop.
   ○ teach me how to hop!
   ○ teach me how to hop.

5. ○ Hop backward like this.
   ○ Hop backward like this!
   ○ hop backward like this.

Common and Proper Nouns

> **Common nouns** name people, places and things. They do not begin with a capital letter. **Proper nouns** have special names and begin with capital letters.

Read each sentence. Circle the common nouns.

1.   The boy makes a boat.

2.   The brothers go to the park.

3.   A girl is with her mother.

4.   A woman sits on a bench.

5.   There are many ducks in the pond.

Write the common nouns you circled under the correct heading.

People	**Places**	**Things**
_____	_____	_____
_____	_____	_____
_____	_____	_____
_____		

Common and Proper Nouns

Read each sentence. Draw a line under each proper noun.

1. Jim and his friends go to the Kentucky Zoo.

2. Sarah sees giraffes and elephants at the zoo.

3. Mark and Tim eat burgers at Snorky's Snackshop.

4. Pete brings Parky along. It is Pete's dog.

5. They see many animals and people at the Kentucky Zoo.

Complete the table below with the correct common and proper nouns from the sentences above.

Common Nouns	Proper Nouns

Date: _____

Common and Proper Nouns

Look at the underlined word in each sentence. Fill in the bubble next to the correct answer.

1. <u>Cary</u> sees a big rat.

   ○ proper noun   ○ common noun

2. Go to Park Lake and look at the <u>flowers</u>.

   ○ proper noun   ○ common noun

3. They saw the <u>Angel Falls</u>, the highest waterfall in the world.

   ○ proper noun   ○ common noun

4. Dad drove the <u>van</u> to the Botanic Gardens.

   ○ proper noun   ○ common noun

5. Please send the letter to <u>Mr Carson</u>.

   ○ proper noun   ○ common noun

6. Seal the <u>envelope</u> and write his name, Mr Timms, on it.

   ○ proper noun   ○ common noun

Singular and Plural Nouns

> Many nouns add **−s** to show more than one. Nouns that end in **s**, **x**, **ch** or **sh** add **−es** to show more than one.

Read each set of sentences. Underline the singular nouns and circle the plural nouns.

1. We have two pianos, a guitar and a drum set in our house.

2. Grandma grows many plants in our garden. There are roses, orchids and fruit trees.

3. Grandpa likes to keep stamps and watches. He keeps them all in his cupboard.

4. Our cat likes biscuits. He plays with a little ball and chews my shoes.

Date: _____

Singular and Plural Nouns

Complete each sentence. Add *–s* or *–es* to the noun in brackets to make it plural.

1. Dad made ten cheese _____. (sandwich)

2. He packed five _____ for the children. (lunch)

3. Lisa put fruit in all the _____. (lunchbox)

4. She packed some paper _____, too. (dish)

5. Gerald packed the _____. (drink)

6. He also brought some _____. (game)

7. Daphne and Lisa put on their best _____. (dress)

8. They also brought some _____. (umbrella)

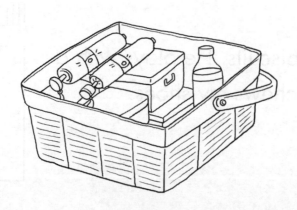

Date: _____

Singular and Plural Nouns

Complete the table below with the correct singular or plural noun.

Singular Nouns	Plural Nouns
park	
	bananas
tree	
fox	
	wishes
bench	
coat	
dish	
	paints
	forks
bottle	
toy	
sketch	
seat	

Countable and Uncountable Nouns

Things that can be counted are **countable nouns**. Things that cannot be counted are **uncountable nouns**.

Underline the countable nouns and circle the uncountable nouns in the sentences below.

1. There are many windows in the classrooms.

2. How many bottles of juice are there?

3. Pass me some milk and two muffins, please.

4. The roads are very slippery after the rain.

5. Our neighbors are very friendly.

6. I enjoy my piano lessons very much.

7. I like making castles in the sand!

8. Our teachers have prepared a wonderful party for us.

Date: _____

Countable and Uncountable Nouns

Decide if the underlined word or words in each sentence are countable or uncountable nouns. Write *C* for countable and *UC* for uncountable on the lines in brackets.

1. The table is stacked with <u>homework</u>. (_____)

2. Let's play a few more <u>games</u> of badminton. (_____)

3. Shannon is afraid of any <u>insect</u> that flies. (_____)

4. Heather likes to eat strawberries with <u>cream</u>. (_____)

5. I love to lie on the <u>grass</u>! (_____)

6. The lively <u>band</u> plays great music. (_____)

7. May I have some <u>peanut butter</u> on my bread, please? (_____)

8. The furniture store sells many kinds of <u>chairs</u>. (_____)

9. Can you please bring our <u>luggage</u> to the lobby? (_____)

10. Dad likes to have a <u>cup</u> of coffee in the morning. (_____)

Countable and Uncountable Nouns

Fill in the blanks with suitable countable or uncountable nouns from the box. Use each word once.

ball	bottles	food	hair	homework
meat	money	parents	presents	salt
soup	time	trees	water	

1. Mother bought some _____ from the butcher and two _____ of milk.

2. My _____ cheered when I kicked the _____.

3. I cannot buy any _____ to eat, as I have no _____.

4. There were many _____ under those Christmas _____.

5. Kat added some _____ to the vegetable _____.

6. You must drink lots of _____ after exercising.

7. I have so much _____ to do but so little _____!

8. I go to the barber to cut my _____.

Verbs

A **verb** is an action word. It tells what someone or something is doing.

Read each sentence. Underline the verb in each sentence.

1. Ronald runs to the field.

2. Michael wears a batting helmet.

3. He smacks the ball hard.

4. Ronald holds the wrong end of the bat.

5. He misses the ball.

6. Ronald waits in left field.

7. Michael hits the ball far away.

8. He races to the next stop.

Verbs

Complete the sentences below. Use the verbs in the box to help you.

roars	hides	looks
runs	swing	climbs

1. The lion is hungry and it _____ loudly.

2. A deer _____ away quickly across the plains.

3. A little rabbit _____ deep in its burrow. It is afraid of the lion.

4. The lion _____ around for food, but it does not see any other animals.

5. The squirrel _____ up the tree and stays there.

6. Only the monkeys are active. They _____ from tree to tree.

Date: _____

Verbs

Look at the underlined word in each sentence. Fill in the bubble to tell if it is a verb.

1. The dog <u>runs</u> down the road.
    ○ Yes   ○ No

2. The girl chases after the <u>dog</u>.
    ○ Yes   ○ No

3. The dog finds a <u>bone</u>.
    ○ Yes   ○ No

4. The dog <u>digs</u> a hole.
    ○ Yes   ○ No

5. The dog hides the bone in the <u>ground</u>.
    ○ Yes   ○ No

6. The girl <u>finds</u> the dog.
    ○ Yes   ○ No

7. Rain starts to fall from the <u>sky</u>.
    ○ Yes   ○ No

8. The girl and the dog <u>play</u> in the rain.
    ○ Yes   ○ No

Simple Sentences

A **simple sentence** tells a complete thought.

Read each group of words. Put an *X* next to each complete thought.

1. One day thirsty _____

2. The crow could not get a drink. _____

3. The crow found a bottle of water. _____

4. Too little water _____

5. Cannot reach _____

6. The crow had a good idea. _____

7. Pebbles in the bottle _____

8. The water rose. _____

9. The crow drank the water. _____

Simple Sentences

Read the sentences. Fill in the blanks using the phrases in the box.

her school bag	She closes	her shoes
all the way to school		

1. Ginny carries _____.

2. Then, she wears _____.

3. _____ the door.

4. Then, she walks _____.

Write two simple sentences about the picture below.

_____

_____

Date: _____

Simple Sentences

Read each group of words. Fill in the bubble next to the complete sentence.

1. ○ The prince and princess
    ○ met at the ball
    ○ The prince and princess met at the ball.

2. ○ all night
    ○ dance all night
    ○ They danced all night.

3. ○ They
    ○ for hours
    ○ They talked for hours.

4. ○ The princess
    ○ The princess had to go.
    ○ had to go

5. ○ drove her home
    ○ The prince
    ○ The prince drove her home.

6. ○ her earrings
    ○ lost
    ○ She lost her earrings.

Word Order

> Words in a sentence must be in an order that makes sense.

Read each group of words. Write the words in the correct order.

1. two brothers can the live together

    _____

2. older brother the a new house finds

    _____

3. they their mother ask to stay with them

    _____

4. who the furniture moved

    _____

5. Max the furniture helps to move

    _____

6. is new house where the

    _____

Word Order

Read each group of words. Write each group of words as a statement and as a question.

1. your pumpkin   that   is

   Statement: _____

   Question: _____

2. help   cut   you   can   pumpkin   the

   Statement: _____

   Question: _____

3. is   the   ripe   pumpkin

   Statement: _____

   Question: _____

4. the   pumpkin   can   we   now   eat

   Statement: _____

   Question: _____

Date: _____

Word Order

Read each group of words. If the word order does not make sense, fill in the bubble next to the correct word order. If the words are in an order that makes sense, fill in the last bubble.

1. Dad made breakfast eggs for.

   ○ Made for breakfast Dad eggs.
   ○ Dad made eggs for breakfast.
   ○ Correct as is

2. Open eggs four he cracked.

   ○ He cracked eggs open four.
   ○ He cracked open four eggs.
   ○ Correct as is

3. Like eggs do you?

   ○ Do you like eggs?   ○ Eggs do you like?
   ○ Correct as is

4. Help you did him?

   ○ Did you help him?   ○ Did him you help?
   ○ Correct as is

5. With fork a beat eggs.

   ○ Beat eggs with a fork.   ○ A fork beat with eggs.
   ○ Correct as is

Present Continuous Tense

We use the **present continuous tense** to talk about something that is happening now. We use **am / is / are** + the verb ending with **-ing** to form the present continuous tense.

Read each sentence. Underline the words in the present continuous form.

1. The children are playing in the field.

2. The clouds are moving quickly.

3. The ball is bouncing away.

4. Only Penny is reading a book.

5. Buster is running after the children.

Read each pair of sentences. Fill in the bubble next to the correct sentence.

6. ○ She is pouring the milk in the cup.
    ○ She are pouring the milk in the cup.

7. ○ They are building a tower with their toy blocks.
    ○ They is building a tower with their toy blocks.

Present Continuous Tense

Fill in the blanks with the present continuous form of the verb in brackets.

1. Gina _____ (look) for her scissors.

2. The boys _____ (help) her to look for them.

3. Grant _____ (blow) the balloons.

4. Peter _____ (bake) the cake.

5. They _____ (wrap) the present.

6. Cheryl and Candice are _____ (put) up the decorations.

7. They _____ (wait) for the birthday girl to return home.

8. They _____ (hide) behind the furniture.

Present Continuous Tense

Fill in the bubble next to the words that correctly complete each sentence.

1. Macy _____ in her room.

   ○ is hiding   ○ are hiding   ○ am hiding

2. Karen _____ for her.

   ○ is looking   ○ are looking   ○ am looking

3. I _____ them play hide-and-seek.

   ○ is watching   ○ are watching   ○ am watching

4. Jem and Jenas _____ on the floor.

   ○ is crawling   ○ are crawling   ○ am crawling

5. You _____ in the corner.

   ○ is sleeping   ○ are sleeping   ○ am sleeping

6. Dad _____ his coffee.

   ○ is drinking   ○ are drinking   ○ am drinking

7. Mum _____ on her puzzle.

   ○ is working   ○ are working   ○ am working

8. Our silly hamster _____ its food.

   ○ is chewing   ○ are chewing   ○ am chewing

Past Tense Verbs

We add **-ed** to most verbs to tell about actions that happened in the past.

Read each sentence. Draw a line under the past tense form of the verb. Then, write the base form of the verb on the line.

1. Last year, Daisy planted some seeds. _____

2. Florence watered the garden every day. _____

3. Together they picked out the weeds. _____

4. They showered the garden with lots of love. _____

5. The flowers bloomed beautifully. _____

6. They watched the flowers for many days. _____

7. They plucked the flowers. _____

8. They placed the flowers in a vase. _____

Past Tense Verbs

Read the first sentence in each pair. Change the underlined verb to tell about the past.

1. Today my dogs <u>push</u> open the back door.

   Yesterday my dogs _____ open the back door.

2. Today they <u>splash</u> in the rain puddles.

   Last night, they _____ in the rain puddles.

3. Now they <u>roll</u> in the mud.

   Last week, they _____ in the mud.

4. Today I <u>follow</u> my dogs' footprints.

   Last Sunday, I _____ my dogs' footprints.

5. Now I <u>wash</u> my dogs from head to toe.

   Earlier I _____ my dogs from head to toe.

Write a sentence using one of the verbs you wrote.

_____

_____

Date: _____

Past Tense Verbs

Read each sentence. Fill in the bubble next to the correct form of the verb that completes each sentence.

1. Last week, I _____ John in the hospital.

   ○ visited   ○ visit

2. Two weeks ago, we _____ up the hill.

   ○ walked   ○ walk

3. That week, he _____ his ankle.

   ○ sprained   ○ sprain

4. He _____ many days in the hospital.

   ○ stayed   ○ stay

5. Today we _____ on the phone.

   ○ talked   ○ talk

6. I _____ a program as I talk to him.

   ○ watched   ○ watch

Irregular Verbs *go* and *do*

Irregular verbs change their spelling when they tell about the past. **Did** is the past tense form of **do** and **does**. **Went** is the past tense form of **go** and **goes**.

Read each sentence. Write *present* if the underlined verb tells about action now. Write *past* if the underlined verb tells about action in the past.

Present	Past
go, goes	went
do, does	did

1. Grace <u>goes</u> to the playground.   _____

2. Some other children <u>go</u>, too.   _____

3. Grace <u>does</u> a scene from a story.   _____

4. The children <u>do</u> the scene with her.   _____

5. Grace <u>went</u> into battle as Joan of Arc.   _____

6. She also <u>did</u> many other parts.   _____

Irregular Verbs *go* and *do*

Choose a verb from the table to complete each sentence.

Present	Past
go, goes	went
do, does	did

1. Last week, our family _____ to the art museum.

2. We _____ the paintings last month.

3. She _____ for art classes every day.

4. My brother and I _____ for art classes every day too.

5. Mark always _____ his homework after class.

6. We _____ our work together today.

Date: _____

Irregular Verbs *go* and *do*

Fill in the bubble next to the word that completes each sentence.

1. Rose _____ to the ballet.

   ○ go   ○ did   ○ goes

2. Two dancers _____ a kick and a turn.

   ○ do   ○ does   ○ goes

3. Another dancer _____ a hop and a jump.

   ○ went   ○ does   ○ do

4. They _____ around in circles very fast.

   ○ goes   ○ did   ○ go

5. Rose _____ home feeling very happy.

   ○ went   ○ does   ○ go

6. She _____ some of the steps too.

   ○ goes   ○ did   ○ go

The Verb *Be* – *Was* and *Were*

Remember that **am**, **is** and **are** are present tense forms of the verb **be**. The words **was** and **were** are forms of the verb **be** that tell about things in the past.

Read each sentence. Underline the verb in each sentence.

1. The girl was unhappy.

2. The boys were at school yesterday.

3. They were at the pet shop.

4. The lion was in the cage.

Read each sentence. Write the word *now* if the action is happening in the present. Write the word *then* if the action happened in the past.

5. The waiter was sick last week.   _____

6. She is at home today.   _____

7. The princes were in Europe last month.   _____

8. The sisters are in the playground.   _____

The Verb *Be* – *Was* and *Were*

We use **was** with singular nouns or the pronouns **he**, **she** or **it**. We use **were** with plural nouns or the pronouns **you**, **we** or **they**.

Complete each sentence with *was* or *were*.

1. They _____ at the park all morning.

2. The cat _____ asleep on the mat.

3. He _____ at the stadium yesterday.

4. We _____ at the zoo on Monday.

Choose a verb from the box to complete each sentence.

am	is	are	was	were

5. I _____ alone at home today.

6. She _____ the only one here.

7. They _____ on vacation last week.

8. He _____ with them last Monday.

9. We _____ off to the zoo now.

Date: _____

The Verb *Be* – *Was* and *Were*

Read each sentence. Fill in the bubble next to the correct word that completes each sentence.

1. You _____ in my class last year.

   ○ was   ○ were   ○ are

2. We _____ classmates again this year.

   ○ was   ○ were   ○ are

3. I _____ in the seat behind you this year.

   ○ was   ○ is   ○ am

4. They _____ the students who arrived today.

   ○ is   ○ were   ○ are

5. She _____ our teacher last year.

   ○ was   ○ were   ○ are

6. Mr Ottie _____ our teacher now.

   ○ is   ○ was   ○ are

There + Be

The word *there*, with forms of the verb *be*, is used to describe what, where, when and how much something is.

Fill in the blanks with *there* + *is/are/was/were*.

1. _____ a football match yesterday afternoon.

2. _____ so many people at the bazaar now!

3. "_____ something you can help me with," said Marty.

4. _____ running tracks beside the river seven years ago.

5. This is strange! _____ a man standing here just now.

6. "_____ about thirty cupcakes in each box," counted the baker.

7. _____ nothing good on television right now.

8. _____ some paper clips in the box last week.

There + Be

Answer the following questions with statements that begin with forms of *there + be*.

1. Are there many animals at the zoo now?

    _____

2. Are there stray cats wandering around here?

    _____

3. Is there a performance this Friday?

    _____

4. Was there a lot of rain yesterday?

    _____

5. Was there a celebration at Edwin's house last week?

    _____

6. Were there many people at the party?

    _____

Date: _____

There + Be

Form sentences using *there + is/are/was/were*. Use the words in brackets to help you.

1. (pies, box, Tuesday)

   _____

2. (guests, Selina's house, today)

   _____

3. (swan, swimming, lake)

   _____

4. (children, feeding, parrots)

   _____

5. (work, do, garage)

   _____

6. (thirsty boys, field)

   _____

Have, Has and Had

We use **have** or **has** to tell about the present. **Have** is usually used with plural nouns. **Has** is used with singular nouns. We use **had** to tell about the past.

Read each sentence. Fill in the bubble next to the word that correctly completes each sentence.

1. Peter Patter _____ many special friends.

   ○ has   ○ have

2. He _____ a cat and a rooster.

   ○ has   ○ have

3. He _____ a toy lion called Rar too.

   ○ has   ○ have

4. Last year, he _____ a smelly bolster, Boo.

   ○ had   ○ has

5. His sister _____ many friends too.

   ○ had   ○ has

6. They _____ a lot of fun playing with their friends.

   ○ have   ○ has

7. Last week, they _____ a party together.

   ○ had   ○ have

Have, Has and Had

Complete each sentence with *have*, *has* or *had*.

1. The man _____ many people in his restaurant last week.

2. Last week, he _____ ten tables.

3. Now, he _____ twenty tables.

4. Last week, only his son _____ time to help him.

5. Today, his daughter _____ time to help too.

6. The children _____ fun setting the tables together.

7. They _____ a good time making the salads earlier in the morning too.

8. The man _____ time to talk to his customers today.

Date: _____

Have, Has and Had

Read each sentence. Fill in the bubble next to the correct word.

1. I _____ a pet bird.

   ○ has   ○ have   ○ had

2. Now, she _____ big white wings.

   ○ has   ○ have   ○ had

3. Earlier, she _____ little white wings.

   ○ has   ○ have   ○ had

4. The baby bird _____ closed eyes when it was born.

   ○ has   ○ have   ○ had

5. Now, the bird _____ big open eyes.

   ○ has   ○ have   ○ had

6. The mother and baby birds _____ fun now.

   ○ has   ○ have   ○ had

7. The baby birds _____ little wings now.

   ○ has   ○ have   ○ had

8. They _____ even smaller wings when they
   were born.

   ○ has   ○ have   ○ had

Direct and Indirect Objects

A **direct object** follows from the verb in a sentence. Direct object sentences answer 'what' or 'who' questions.

Example: What did Maggie write? (letter)
| subject | + | verb | + | direct object |
| Maggie | + | wrote | + | a letter. |

Answer the following questions using the direct objects in brackets.

1. What does Gerald play with? (toy car)

    _____

2. What did Aaron look at? (a flock of birds)

    _____

3. Where did our father go? (the office)

    _____

4. What does the store sell? (pet food)

    _____

5. Who did she play with? (Megan)

    _____

Direct and Indirect Objects

The person or thing that receives the direct object is the **indirect object**. Indirect object sentences answer 'to whom' or 'for whom' questions.

Example: To whom did Maggie write a letter? (Leonard)

subject + verb + indirect object + direct object

Maggie + wrote + Leonard + a letter.

Answer the following questions using the indirect objects in brackets.

1. To whom did you give the invitation? (Ursula)

   _____

2. For whom did you play the piano? (brother)

   _____

3. For whom did Grandma bake the cookies? (us)

   _____

4. For whom did you tape the show? (Christopher)

   _____

5. For whom did Spencer make a card? (his teacher)

   _____

Direct and Indirect Objects

Circle the indirect objects and underline the direct objects in the sentences below.

1. June gave Kelsey some marbles.

2. Laurence jumped on the trampoline.

3. Kent brought his brother some toys.

4. Tiffany spoke to Charles.

5. Mrs Harris took a bus to town.

6. We promised Uncle Phillip good results.

7. Mr Roberts bought his children a train set.

8. The plane landed at the airport.

Subject-Verb Agreement

If the subject of a sentence refers to one thing, we often add **-s** to the verb. If the subject refers to more than one, we do not add **-s**.

Circle the correct form of the verb in brackets.

1. Kim (write / writes) a story about a monkey.

2. The monkey (meet / meets) his friend in the city.

3. The monkeys (shop / shops) for toys and presents.

4. The store (close / closes) at 7 o'clock.

5. The monkeys (forget / forgets) the time.

6. The owner (lock / locks) the doors.

7. The friends (bang / bangs) on the window.

8. Many people (call / calls) for help.

9. Finally, the monkeys (hear / hears) the door open.

Subject-Verb Agreement

Complete each sentence with the correct form of the verb in brackets.

1. Two baby llamas _____ (play) in the mountains.

2. One baby llama _____ (hide) under a bush.

3. The baby animals _____ (chase) flying leaves.

4. Soon the mother llama _____ (call) them.

5. The babies _____ (run) to her.

6. The two babies _____ (stand) next to their mother.

7. One baby _____ (close) its eyes.

8. The mother llama _____ (nudge) the baby gently.

9. But the baby llama _____ (sleep).

10. Soon both baby llamas _____ (sleep).

Date: _____

Subject-Verb Agreement

Read the sentences. Fill in the bubble next to the word that correctly completes each sentence.

1. Two friends _____ beautiful bead necklaces.

    ○ makes   ○ make

2. One girl _____ some pieces of string.

    ○ cut   ○ cuts

3. The girls _____ red, blue and yellow beads.

    ○ use   ○ uses

4. The yellow beads _____ in the dark.

    ○ glows   ○ glow

5. The necklaces _____ from the rod.

    ○ hang   ○ hangs

6. The boys _____ a necklace for their mother.

    ○ buy   ○ buys

7. One boy _____ the short necklace with round beads.

    ○ pick   ○ picks

8. The girls _____ all the necklaces.

    ○ sell   ○ sells

Pronouns

We use **pronouns**, such as *me*, *you*, *him*, *her*, *it*, *us* and *them*, in place of people or things that we are talking about.

Example: Felix took a pencil from **Geraldine**.

Felix took a pencil from **her**.

Rewrite the sentences below. Replace the underlined objects with the pronouns in brackets.

1. I am going to jog with <u>Chad</u>. (him)

    _____

2. Bernard carried the shopping for <u>Aunt Nancy</u>. (her)

    _____

3. We are going to play against <u>the Morton football team</u>. (them)

    _____

4. Coach Trevor will train <u>our team</u> well. (us)

    _____

5. Please give <u>the dog</u> a bone. (it)

    _____

Pronouns

Rewrite the sentences by replacing the underlined objects with pronouns.

1. Uncle Bob taught <u>my brothers and I</u> to rollerblade.

    _____

2. My brothers were zooming around with <u>Uncle Bob</u>.

    _____

3. As they went past, they waved to <u>Sheila</u>.

    _____

4. I wanted to zip around like <u>my brothers</u>.

    _____

5. Instead, I fell over <u>a huge rock</u>.

    _____

    _____

Pronouns

Write the correct pronouns in the blanks below.

Danny walked into a florist. "Hello! May I help 1._____?"

the salesgirl called out cheerily. "Yes, please," replied Danny.

"It is my mother's birthday. I want to buy some flowers for 2.

_____."

"How about those roses? I just got 3. _____ this morning,"

suggested the salesgirl. "How much would a bouquet cost?"

asked Danny.

"4._____ costs only twenty dollars for a dozen roses,"

smiled the salesgirl. "That's great! I'll take a dozen," said Danny.

"Please deliver the roses to my mother on my behalf and tell

5. _____ that they are from 6. _____. Thank

7. _____ very much!"

Adjectives

An **adjective** describes a person, place or thing. Color, size and number words are adjectives.

Read each sentence. Underline the nouns. Then, circle the adjective that tells about each noun.

1. The brown donkey carried the heavy sack.

2. The striped cat chased two birds.

3. The little rooster crowed six times.

4. The furry rabbit ate its sweet carrots.

Write the adjectives from the sentences above.

5. Write the adjectives that tell what kind.

   _____

6. Write the adjectives that tell how many.

   _____

Adjectives

Read each sentence. Write the adjective on the line and circle the noun it describes.

1. Peggy and Rosa went to the big zoo. _____

2. They looked up at the tall giraffe. _____

3. The giraffe looked at the two girls. _____

4. The giraffe had brown spots. _____

5. The giraffe ate the green leaves. _____

6. There were three baby giraffes. _____

Write adjectives from the sentences in the table below.

Color Adjectives	Size Adjectives	Number Adjectives

Date: _____

Adjectives

Read each sentence. Fill in the bubble next to the adjective.

1. In the morning, Jenny put on red boots.

    ○ put   ○ boots   ○ red   ○ on

2. She found a yellow hat in the closet.

    ○ She   ○ hat   ○ found   ○ yellow

3. She opened her purple umbrella.

    ○ opened   ○ She   ○ umbrella   ○ purple

4. Jenny walked past a big house.

    ○ big   ○ house   ○ walked   ○ past

5. She waved to three friends.

    ○ waved   ○ three   ○ to   ○ friends

6. A little puppy trotted behind her.

    ○ little   ○ puppy   ○ trotted   ○ behind

7. She jumped over a huge puddle.

    ○ She   ○ jumped   ○ huge   ○ puddle

8. Two birds took a drink of water.

    ○ birds   ○ took   ○ water   ○ Two

Date: _____

Prepositions

> **Prepositions** tell where and when something or someone is.
> Example: The giraffe is **in** the zoo.
> I will be there **at** six o'clock.

Fill in the blanks with suitable prepositions from the box.

above	at	from	in
on	to	through	under

1. Let's go to the beach _____ Saturday.

2. Would you like to go _____ the amusement park today?

3. The birds are flying _____ the trees.

4. The children like to hide _____ the bed.

5. We are going to the concert _____ the evening.

6. You need to walk _____ the forest to get to the other side.

7. I will be going to your house _____ school.

8. We are meeting James _____ four in the afternoon.

68

Prepositions

Fill in the blanks with suitable prepositions of your own.

1. Melanie looks very pretty _____ this photograph.

2. The sun is the hottest _____ summer.

3. Let's go _____ the living room to play some board games.

4. My father usually works till late _____ night.

5. Mom is talking to Aunt Annie _____ the phone.

6. We will be here _____ the whole day.

7. Our neighbors have been on vacation _____ last week.

8. Hugh is sitting _____ the chair.

Date: _____

Prepositions

Answer the following questions using the words in brackets and suitable prepositions.

1. When will Remus come again? (November)

   _____

2. Where shall I meet you? (library)

   _____

3. When is Mrs Timms having a celebration? (Tuesday)

   _____

4. Where shall I place the box? (Cassie's room)

   _____

5. Where do you go for dance classes? (Cedar Street)

   _____

6. When will the History test be? (9 February)

   _____

Revision

Rewrite the questions below using the correct punctuation. Then, answer the questions using complete sentences. Begin your answers with *yes* or *no* and end them with a period or exclamation mark.

1. have you ever seen the milky way

    Question: _____

    Answer: _____

2. did you enjoy yourself at the christmas party

    Question: _____

    Answer: _____

3. are you watching star wars at the cinema

    Question: _____

    Answer: _____

4. will you be going to the sydney opera house

    Question: _____

    Answer: _____

5. were you tired after the new year parade

    Question: _____

    Answer: _____

Form commands with the words in brackets. Use appropriate punctuation and correct forms of the verbs.

6. (meet, us, yellowstone park)

_____

7. (turn right, bigsave shopping mall)

_____

8. (stop, push, jimmy)

_____

9. (bring, sister, cathy's house, tonight)

_____

10. (order, pizza, jefferson street)

_____

Read each sentence. Fill in the bubble next to the word that correctly completes each sentence.

11. The _____ writes his name on the page.

   ○ boy   ○ boys

12. The woodcutters _____ their axes to chop the trees.

   ○ use   ○ uses

13. The _____ are chirping in the nests.

   ○ birds   ○ bird

14. The tennis player _____ her shoelaces.

   ○ tie   ○ ties

15. Tabitha's _____ send her presents.

   ○ friends   ○ friend

16. The boys _____ in the garden.

   ○ plays   ○ play

17. The children _____ in class.

   ○ is   ○ are

18. Jenny _____ down the stairs.

   ○ falls   ○ fall

Rearrange the words to form simple sentences.

19. the   ate   Bryan   cake

   _____

20. balloons   I   playing   love   with

   _____

21. thief   the   policemen   catch   the

   _____

Read each sentence. Fill in the bubble next to the word that correctly completes each sentence.

22. The fairy felt sorry for the poor man and _____ him a wish.

    ○ grants   ○ granted

23. The poor man _____ so happy that he cried.

    ○ was   ○ is

24. The man now _____ other poor people.

    ○ helps   ○ helped

25. He _____ some poor people today.

    ○ is meeting   ○ met

26. He _____ to help them.

    ○ wants   ○ wanted

27. The poor people _____ grateful for his help.

    ○ are   ○ were

28. He _____ to the supermarket to get food for them yesterday.

    ○ go   ○ went

Underline the indirect objects in the sentences. Rewrite the sentences by replacing them with suitable pronouns.

29. I threw Chris a ball.

_____

30. Dad bought Esther new shoes.

_____

31. She brought her parrot to the vet.

_____

32. I gave Janice and Jane some chocolate.

_____

33. Harry told my brother and me to go home.

_____

Fill in the blanks with suitable forms of verbs and prepositions of place and time.

34. There _____ delicious muffins _____ the box.

35. There _____ a small box _____ the room.

36. _____ there any red apples _____ the table?

37. There _____ beautiful decorations hanging _____ the ceiling.

Answer Key

Page 5
1. T   2. Q   3. Q   4. T
5. T   6. Q   7. T

Page 6
1. Where is James?
2. James is in the classroom.
3. He is helping Miss Lina clean the board.
4. Who is the one sweeping the floor?
5. That is Monica.
6. She is our class monitor.

Page 7
1. correct as is   2. cats.   3. Do you
4. correct as is   5. correct as is   6. correct as is
7. like?   8. correct as is

Page 8
1. Yes   2. Yes   3. Yes
4. No   5. Yes   6. No

Page 9
1. Do you want to visit Grandma this weekend?
2. Will you be going swimming?
3. Is the book interesting?
4. Would you like to pet my dog?
5. Did you see Benson at lunch?
6. Shall we have pizza tomorrow evening?
7. Has Jaden gone home yet?
8. Should I turn off the light?

Page 10
1. Yes, we shall celebrate Mom's birthday.
2. No, I will not be watching the football game.
3. Yes, Carlson is going to Vancouver with his parents.
4. No, I am not listening to the radio.
5. Yes, there is milk in the refrigerator.
6. Yes, you may speak to Mr Raye.

Page 11
1. The first day of January is New Year's Day.
2. What special dish do we eat during Thanksgiving?
3. Our school celebrates Teacher's Day with a party.
4. I am preparing a scary-looking costume for Halloween.
5. Did you play tricks on your friends on April Fool's Day?
6. They are decorting the house for Christmas.

Page 12
1. On Mother's Day, I will give my mother roses.
2. There is no school on Children's Day.
3. We will have a party on New Year's Eve.
4. I will make breakfast for my father on Father's Day.
5. On National Day, we fly our country's flag.
6. On Chinese New Year, there will be fireworks.

Page 13
Ensure the following words have capital letters:
Superbowl, Arizona International Conference, Good
Friday, Easter

Page 14
Ensure each exclamation mark is circled and the
capital letter at the beginning of each new sentence
is underlined.
4. Oh my! The whole house is wet!
5. Run! They are catching up!
6. Surprise! Happy Birthday!

Page 15
1. Run to the show!
2. Oh my, I'm very late!
3. What a great show!
4. Watch out, the floor is wet!
5. Wow, we had lots of fun!

Page 16
1. Yes! The cow gave birth to a calf!
2. Oh no! There is a rat in my house!
3. That boy is so naughty!
4. The pot is hot!
5. Watch out! There is a hole in the ground!
6. That baby cries so loudly! Stop that baby from crying!

Page 17
1. C   2. E   3. C
4. E   5. E
6. Be yourself!   7. Copy this page ten times.

Page 18
1. fear   2. excitement   3. surprise
4. anger   5. Change out of your clothes now.
6. Keep quiet.

Page 19

1. You are my best friend in the world!
2. The picture is beautiful!
3. We did it!
4. Teach me how to hop.
5. Hop backward like this.

Page 20

1. boy, boat   2. brothers, park   3. girl, mother
4. woman, bench 5. ducks, pond
People: boy, brothers, girl, mother, woman
Places: park, pond
Things: boat, bench

Page 21

1. Jim, Kentucky Zoo   2. Sarah
3. Mark, Tim, Snorky's Snackshop
4. Pete, Parky   5. Kentucky Zoo
Common nouns: friends, giraffes, elephants, zoo,
burgers, dog, animals, people
Proper nouns: Jim, Kentucky Zoo, Sarah, Mark, Tim,
Snorky's Snackshop, Pete, Parky

Page 22

1. Proper noun   2. Common noun
3. Proper noun   4. Common noun
5. Proper noun   6. Common noun

Page 23

1. Underline: house, guitar, drum set; Circle: pianos
2. Underline: Grandma, garden; Circle: plants, roses,
   orchids, fruit trees.
3. Underline: Grandpa, cupboard; Circle: stamps,
   watches
4. Underline: cat, ball; Circle: biscuits, shoes

Page 24

1. sandwiches   2. lunches   3. lunchboxes
4. dishes   5. drinks   6. games
7. dresses   8. umbrellas

Page 25

park – parks   banana – bananas
tree – trees   fox – foxes
wish – wishes   bench – benches
coat – coats   dish – dishes
paint – paints   fork – forks
bottle – bottles   toy – toys
sketch – sketches   seat – seats

Page 26

1. Underline: windows, classrooms
2. Underline: bottles; Circle: juice
3. Underline: muffins; Circle: milk
4. Underline: roads; Circle: rain

5. Underline: neighbors
6. Underline: piano lessons
7. Underline: castles; Circle: sand
8. Underline: teachers, party

Page 27

1. UC   2. C   3. C   4. UC
5. UC   6. C   7. UC   8. C
9. C   10. C

Page 28

1. meat, bottles   2. parents, ball
3. food, money   4. presents, trees
5. salt, soup   6. water
7. homework, time   8. hair

Page 29

1. runs   2. wears   3. smacks
4. holds   5. misses   6. waits
7. hits   8. races

Page 30

1. roars   2. runs   3. hides
4. looks   5. climbs   6. swing

Page 31

1. Yes   2. No   3. No
4. Yes   5. No   6. Yes
7. No   8. Yes

Page 32

Put an X next to sentences 2, 3, 6, 8 and 9.

Page 33

1. Ginny carries her school bag.
2. Then, she wears her shoes.
3. She closes the door.
4. Then, she walks all the way to school.
Accept all reasonable answers.

Page 34

1. The prince and princess met at the ball.
2. They danced all night.
3. They talked for hours.
4. The princess had to go.
5. The prince drove her home.
6. She lost her earrings.

Page 35

1. The two brothers can live together.
2. The older brother finds a new house.
3. They ask their mother to stay with them.
4. Who moved the furniture?
5. Max helps to move the furniture.
6. Where is the new house?

Page 36
1. That is your pumpkin. / Is that your pumpkin?
2. You can help cut the pumpkin. / Can you help cut the pumpkin?
3. The pumpkin is ripe. / Is the pumpkin ripe?
4. We can eat the pumpkin now. / Can we eat the pumpkin now?

Page 37
1. Dad made eggs for breakfast.
2. He cracked open four eggs.
3. Do you like eggs?
4. Did you help him?
5. Beat eggs with a fork.

Page 38
1. are playing   2. are moving   3. is bouncing
4. is reading   5. is running
6. She is pouring the milk in the cup.
7. They are building a tower with their toy blocks.

Page 39
1. is looking   2. are helping   3. is blowing
4. is baking   5. are wrapping   6. are putting
7. are waiting   8. are hiding

Page 40
1. is hiding   2. is looking   3. am watching
4. are crawling   5. are sleeping   6. is drinking
7. is working   8. is chewing

Page 41
1. <u>planted</u> / plant   2. <u>watered</u> / water
3. <u>picked</u> / pick   4. <u>showered</u> / shower
5. <u>bloomed</u> / bloom   6. <u>watched</u> / watch
7. <u>plucked</u> / pluck   8. <u>placed</u> / place

Page 42
1. pushed   2. splashed   3. rolled
4. followed   5. washed
Accept all reasonable answers.

Page 43
1. visited   2. walked   3. sprained
4. stayed   5. talk   6. watch

Page 44
1. present   2. present   3. present
4. present   4. past   5. past

Page 45
1. went   2. did   3. goes
4. go   5. does 6. do

Page 46
1. goes   2. do   3. does
4. go   5. went   6. did

Page 47
1. was   2. were   3. were
4. was   5. then   6. now
7. then   8. now

Page 48
1. were   2. was   3. was
4. were   5. am   6. is
7. were   8. was   9. are

Page 49
1. were   2. are   3. am
4. are   5. was   6. is

Page 50
1. There was   2. There are   3. There is
4. There were   5. There was   6. There are
7. There is   8. There were

Page 51
1. There are many animals at the zoo now.
2. There are stray cats wandering around here.
3. There is a performance on Friday.
4. There was a lot of rain yesterday.
5. There was a celebration at Edwin's house last week.
6. There were many people at the party.

Page 52
These are suggested answers.
1. There were pies in the box on Tuesday.
2. There are guests at Selina's house today.
3. There is a swan swimming in the lake.
4. There are children feeding the parrots.
5. There is work to do in the garage.
6. There are thirsty boys on the field.

Page 53
1. has   2. has   3. has   4. had
5. has   6. have 7. had   8. has

Page 54
1. had   2. had   3. has   4. had
5. has   6. have 7. have   8. has

Page 55
1. have 2. has   3. had   4. had
5. has   6. have 7. have   8. had

Page 56
1. Gerald plays with a toy car.
2. Aaron looks at a flock of birds.

78

3. Our father went to the office.
4. The store sells pet food.
5. She played with Megan.

Page 57
1. I gave Ursula the invitation.
2. I played the piano for my brother.
3. Grandma baked the cookies for us.
4. I taped the show for Christopher.
5. Spencer made a card for his teacher.

Page 58
1. Circle: Kelsey; Underline: marbles
2. Underline: trampoline
3. Circle: his brother; Underline: toys
4. Underline: Charles
5. Circle: bus; Underline: town
6. Circle: Uncle Phillip; Underline: results
7. Circle: children; Underline: train set
8. Underline: airport

Page 59
1. writes   2. meets   3. shop
4. closes   5. forget   6. locks
7. bang   8. call   9. hear

Page 60
1. play   2. hides   3. chase
4. calls   5. run   6. stand
7. closes   8. nudges   9. sleeps
10. sleep

Page 61
1. make   2. cuts   3. use
4. glow   5. hang   6. buy
7. picks   8. sell

Page 62
1. I am going to jog with him.
2. Bernand carried the shopping for her.
3. We are going to play against them.
4. Coach Trevor will train us well.
5. Please give it a bone.

Page 63
1. Uncle Bob taught us to rollerblade.
2. My brothers were zooming around with him.
3. As they went past, they waved to her.
4. I wanted to zip around like them.
5. Instead, I fell over it.

Page 64
1. you   2. her   3. them   4. It
5. her   6. me   7. you

Page 65
1. Underline: donkey, sack, Circle: brown, heavy
2. Underline: cat, birds, Circle: striped, two
3. Underline: rooster, times, Circle: little, six
4. Underline: rabbit, carrots, Circle: furry, sweet
5. brown, heavy, striped, little, furry, sweet
6. two, six

Page 66
1. Circle: zoo; Write: big
2. Circle: giraffe; Write: tall
3. Circle: girls; Write: two
4. Circle: spots; Write: brown
5. Circle: leaves; Write: green
6. Circle: baby giraffes; Write: three
Color Adjectives: brown, green
Size Adjectives: big, tall
Number Adjectives: two, three

Page 67
1. red   2. yellow   3. purple
4. big   5. three   6. little
7. huge   8. Two

Page 68
1. on   2. to   3. above
4. under   5. in   6. through
7. from   8. at

Page 69
1. in   2. in   3. to
4. at   5. on   6. for
7. since   8. on

Page 70
1. Remus will come again in November.
2. I shall meet you in the library.
3. Mrs Timms is having a celebration on Tuesday.
4. I shall place the box in Cassie's room.
5. I go to dance classes at Cedar Street.
6. The History test will be on 9 February.

Pages 71–75
1. Have you ever seen the Milky Way? / No, I have not seen the Milky Way.
2. Did you enjoy yourself at the Christmas party? / Yes, I enjoyed myself at the Christmas party.
3. Are you watching Star Wars at the cinema? / Yes, I am watching Star Wars at the cinema.
4. Will you be going to the Sydney Opera House? / Yes, I will be going to the Sydney Opera House.
5. Were you tired after the New Year parade? / Yes, I was tired after the New Year parade.
6. Meet us at Yellowstone Park.

7. Turn right at Bigsave shopping mall.
8. Stop pushing Jimmy.
9. Bring your sister to Cathy's house tonight.
10. Order the pizza from Jefferson Street.
11. boy   12. use   13. birds
14. ties   15. friends   16. play
17. are   18. falls
19. Bryan ate the cake.
20. I love playing with balloons.
21. The policemen catch the thief.

22. granted   23. was   24. helps
25. is meeting   26. wants   27. are
28. went
29. Chris: I threw him a ball.
30. Esther: Dad bought her new shoes.
31. her parrot: She brought it to the vet.
32. Janice and Jane: I gave them some chocolate.
33. my brother and I: Harry told us to go home.
34. are, in   35. is, in   36. Are, on
37. are, from

80